Mommy's Little SONshine

Written by
Dr. Sheila R. Thomas

Illustrations: Abhiman Ranaweera

Mommy's Little SONshine

ISBN 978-1-7348870-4-4

Text Copyright © 2021 Dr. Sheila R. Thomas

Illustrations Copyright © Abhiman Ranaweera

All rights reserved.

No part of this book may be reproduced in any form, stored in any retrieval system, or transmitted in any form by any means—electronic, mechanical, photocopy, recording, or otherwise without prior written permission from the publisher.

Published in the United States by Great Day Publishing

This book
is dedicated
to all Moms
and their
little SONshines

Mommy's Little Sonshine, so cute and oh so sweet.

I love to count your fingers and kiss your tiny feet.

Your sweet, sweet cries are like music to my ears.

I will always console you whenever you shed tears.

You are my little SONshine!

I love to hold and hug you while rocking you to sleep.
I sing sweet lullabies while you dream of little sheep.

You are my little SONshine!

Watching you learn and grow is my favorite thing to do. You are my baby boy. There's no other like you.

You are my little SONshine!

I will love you forever and always.
In my heart, you will always be.
You are my little Sonshine and God's special gift to me.

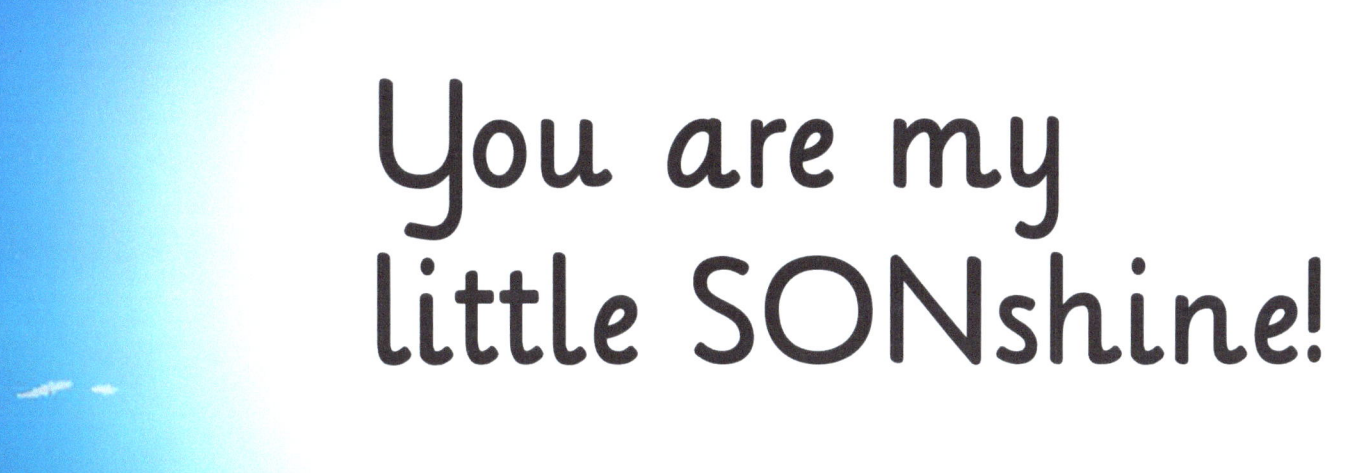

You are my little SONshine!

Author's Bio

Dr. Sheila R. Thomas is the founder of Thomas Educational Consulting and Training and Great Day Publishing. She utilizes her brand to train, facilitate, and educate parents and teachers with curricula and books that she has written. Dr. Thomas is also the author of a children's book, J.R.'s Biggest Fan, a coloring book for boys titled, Yes, I Can, and an inspirational book for women, W.A.I.T.: Women Anticipating Incredible Turnaround. Sheila and her husband, Erick, have three sons, Arenzo, James, and Erick, one grandson, Caleb, and their furbaby, TyTy.

Dr. Sheila R. Thomas